BOUQUET

BOUQUET

PHOTOGRAPHS BY *Doug Benezra* EDITED BY *Pamela Prince*

HARMONY BOOKS NEW YORK

A detailed list of permissions to reprint previously published
material appears on page 80.

Published by Harmony Books, a division of Crown Publishers, Inc.
201 East 50th Street, New York, New York 10022.
Member of the Crown Publishing Group.
Random House, Inc. New York, Toronto, London, Sydney, Auckland
Harmony and colophon are trademarks of Crown Publishers, Inc.
Manufactured in Singapore

Library of Congress Cataloging-in-Publication Data
Bouquet / photographs by Doug Benezra ; edited by Pamela Prince.
  p. cm.
  1. *Flowers--Literary collections.* 2. *Flowers--Pictorial works.*
  I. *Benezra, Doug.* II. *Prince, Pamela.*
PN6071.F5B68 1993   92-34168
808.8'036--dc20   CIP

ISBN 0-517-58520-0
10 9 8 7 6 5 4 3 2 1

First Edition

for Gertrude Benezra [D.B.] *for Dr. Howard Bloom* [P.L.P.]

Go, little book, and wish to all

Flowers in the garden, meat in the hall,

A bin of wine, a spice of wit,

A house with lawns enclosing it,

A living river by the door,

A nightingale in the sycamore!

S

he comes and draws me as a magnet draws filaments of iron

She has the lovely appearance

Of an adorable redhead

Her hair turns golden you would say

A beautiful lightning flash that goes on and on

Or the flames that spread out their feathers

In wilting tea roses...

From "The Pretty Redhead"
GUILLAUME APOLLINAIRE
Translated by James Wright

8

Here comes the time when, vibrating on

noises and perfumes circle in the evening air;

its stem, every flower fumes like a censer;

O melancholy waltz and languid vertigo!

From "Evening Harmony"
Charles Baudelaire

I gazed at Albertine's cheeks
as she spoke, and asked
myself what might be the
perfume, the taste of them:
this time they were not cool,
but glowed with a uniform
pink, violet-tinted, creamy,
like certain roses whose
petals have a waxy gloss.
I felt a passionate
longing for them such as
one feels sometimes for a
particular flower...

From *Within A Budding Grove*
Remembrance of Things Past
MARCEL PROUST

You Among Flowers

The butterfly weed in the terra-cotta vase recalls
the Ozarks... Taneycomo Lake—
and above all,
its coralline sparks against the milkweed milk of your throat and shoulders,
storming the gentle brown of your eyes and hair.

You always held flowers so... in the sheltering curve
of your left arm,
as a child is held—the blossoms miniature copies of your face.

You were loveliest when your face matched small spring flowers,
wild grown, peasant bonneted—
such as it hurts to pick... and hurts to leave alone.

But when you blossomed out variegated, hot-house gardened,
your beauty troubled me—
I saw you as a jewel burning in each stalking eye... and sensed
you were not wholly mine, like a star or a people's song.

From *Never a Greater Need*
WALTER BENTON

The first morning
I woke in surprise to your body
for I had been dreaming it
as I do

all around us white petals had never slept
leaves touched the early light
your breath warm as your skin on my neck
your eyes opening

smell of dew

From *The Compass Flower*
W. S. MERWIN

The lovely days disappear
the lovely holidays
suns and planets
go round in a circle
but you my little one
you go straight
toward you know not what
very slowly draw near
the sudden wrinkle
the weighty fat
the triple chin
the flabby muscle
come gather gather
the roses the roses
roses of life
and may their petals
be a calm sea
of happinesses
come gather gather
if you don't do it
you're fooling yourself
little sweetie little sweetie
you're fooling yourself

From "If You Imagine"
RAYMOND QUENEAU
Translated from the French
by Michael Benedikt

This morning

even my morning glories

are hiding,

not wanting to show

their sleep-mussed hair.

ONO NO KOMACHI
[9TH CENTURY]
Translated from the Japanese
by Jane Hirshfield

The beauty of fading flowers: the petals twist as if under the effect of fire: and of course that's what it really is: a dehydration. They twist so as to expose the seeds to whom they now decide to give their chance, to whom they leave the field free. ❧ This is the season when nature confronts the flower, forcing it to lay itself open to change, to discard itself: it shrivels up, and twists, it shrinks, and gives the victory to the seed which it has made ready, and which emerges from it ❧. Time among the plants is expressed in terms of space, in the space which the plants occupy little by little, filling out patterns which are probably forever determined.... ❧ Like the development of crystals: a will to formation, coupled with an absolute inability to form oneself in any other fashion but the *one*. ❧

From *Flora and Fauna*
FRANCIS PONGE
Translated from the French
by Richard Wilbur

THE ACT

There were the roses, in the rain.

Don't cut them, I pleaded.

They won't last, she said

But they're so beautiful

where they are.

Agh, we were all beautiful once, she

said,

and cut them and gave them to me in my hand.

WILLIAM CARLOS WILLIAMS

The soundless dusk was growing dim
in the midst of a sweet and quiet repose,
and in the blue shadows of the bower
the pallor of moonlight filtered down.

Your hand, all nerves, was stripping
petals from the roses with restless
impatience, which at times the secret
impulse of a desire was urging.

And when you'd picked a white and tender rose,
that was like a trembling bird
caught in your hand by chance,

with cautious step you drew near.
You gave me the rose with your eyes
and I felt the sensation of a kiss.

From *Las lenguas del diamante*, 1919
JUANA DE IBARBOUROU
Translated from the Spanish by Perry Higman

A thing of beauty is a joy forever:
Its loveliness increases; it will never
Pass into nothingness; but still will keep
A bower quiet for us, and a sleep
Full of sweet dreams, and health, and quiet breathing.
Therefore, on every morrow, are we wreathing
A flowery band to bind us to this earth,
Spite of despondence, of the inhuman dearth
Of noble natures, of the gloomy days,
Of all the unhealthy and o'er darken'd ways
Made for our searching: yes, in spite of all,
Some shape of beauty moves away the pall
From our dark spirits. Such the sun, the moon,
Trees old and young, sprouting a shady boon
For simple sheep; and such are daffodils
With the green world they live in....

From *Endymion*
A Romance
JOHN KEATS

Neither that afternoon nor the next did the illustrious Giambattista Marino die, he whom the unanimous mouths of Fame–to use an image dear to him–proclaimed as the new Homer and the new Dante. But the still, noiseless fact that took place then was in reality the last event of his life. Laden with years and with glory, he lay dying on a huge Spanish bed with carved bedposts. It is not hard to imagine a serene balcony a few steps away, facing the west, and, below, marble and laurels and a garden whose various levels are duplicated in a rectangle of water. A woman has placed in a goblet a yellow rose. The man murmurs the inevitable lines that now, to tell the truth, bore even him a little:

> Purple of the garden, pomp of the meadow,
> Gem of spring, April's eye...

Then the revelation occurred: Marino saw the rose as Adam might have seen it in Paradise, and he thought that the rose was to be found in its own eternity and not in his words; and that we may mention or allude to a thing, but not express it; and that the tall, proud volumes casting a golden shadow in a corner were not–as his vanity had dreamed–a mirror of the world, but rather one thing more added to the world.

Marino achieved this illumination on the eve of his death, and Homer and Dante may have achieved it as well.

From *Dreamtigers*
JORGE LUIS BORGES
Translated from El Hacedor
by Mildred Boyer and Harold Morland

After dream,
how real
the iris.

SHUSHIKI
Translated from the Japanese

Oh, this is the joy of the rose:

That it blows,

And goes.

From *In Rose Time*
WILLA CATHER

Bought
  from the flower-peddler's tray
one spring branch
  just open
  in bloom
Droplets
  fleck it evenly
still clouded red
    with a mist of dew
I'm afraid he'll
    take it into his head
that my face is not
    so fair!
    so fair!
In high-
combed hair
  I fasten
  a gold pin
  aslant
There!
let him look
  Let him compare the two

Lɪ Cʜɪɴɢ-ᴄʜᴀᴏ [1084-1151]
*Translated from the Chinese
by C. W. Kwock and Vincent McHugh*

The roses,
mouths of glowing embers,
flames of flesh,
licked at the incorruptibility of the marble...

From "Contes et nouvelles"
RACHILDE
Translated from the French by Daniel Russell

QUEEN ANNE'S LACE

Her body is not so white as
anemone petals nor so smooth—not
so remote a thing. It is a field
of the wild carrot taking
the field by force; the grass
does not raise above it.
Here is no question of whiteness,
white as can be, with a purple mole
at the center of each flower.
Each flower is a hand's span
of her whiteness. Wherever
his hand has lain there is
a tiny purple blemish. Each part
is a blossom under his touch
to which the fibres of her being
stem one by one, each to its end,
until the whole field is a
white desire, empty, a single stem,
a cluster, flower by flower,
a pious wish to whiteness gone over—
or nothing.

WILLIAM CARLOS WILLIAMS

Lady moon light white flowers open in sweet silence

From *Memory Gardens*
Robert Creeley

A single flow'r he sent me, since we met.
　All tenderly his messenger he chose;
Deep-hearted, pure, with scented dew still wet—
　One perfect rose.

I knew the language of floweret;
　"My fragile leaves," it said, "his heart enclose."—
Love long has taken for his amulet
　One perfect rose.

Why is it no one ever sent me yet
　One perfect limousine, do you suppose?
Ah no, it's always just my luck to get
　One perfect rose.

DOROTHY PARKER

Nameless

white poppy whoever looks at you is alone

and when I look at your petals
each time they open

and think of each time
that I have passed them

I know that I have wanted
to say Wait

and why should they

From *The Compass Flower*
W. S. MERWIN

46

If there were no such thing

as cherry blossoms

in this world, in springtime

how untroubled

our hearts would be!

From *On Nunobiki Waterfall*
ARIWARA NO NARIHIRA
[825-880]

I follow the moon into the mountains,

      I search for clouds to accompany me home.

A spring morning, dew on the flowers:

      and the fragrance clings to my gown.

WANG AN-SHIH [1021-1086]
Translated from the Chinese by Jan W. Walls

You ask if you have changed: you have.
As a lover's kiss evokes...evolves...shapes into a child,
so do you move from beauty to beauty –
as a white pear blossom evolves into a golden pear.

And who will choose between a thing of fragrant petals
and one of honeyed curves...for beauty's face?
And as for other delights –
where once the bee sucked sweet . . . now sucks the wasp.
. . . .
We are two vines curved to one another...twined into
one stem –
too like and near to discern the changes of our growing.

From "Of Your Infinite Aspects"
Never a Greater Need
WALTER BENTON

52

She tells her love while half asleep,

In the dark hours,

With half-words whispered low:

As Earth stirs in her winter sleep

And puts out grass and flowers

Despite the snow,

Despite the falling snow.

ROBERT GRAVES

Come quickly—as soon as
these blossoms open,
they fall.
This world exists
as a sheen of dew on flowers.

IZUMI SHIKIBU [974-1034]
*Translated from the Japanese
by Jane Hirshfield*

As certain as color

Passes from the petal,

Irrevocable as flesh,

The gazing eye falls

　　Through the world.

ONO NO KOMACHI
[9TH CENTURY]
*Translated from the Japanese
by Kenneth Rexroth*

He left me all
His black
and his
honey in

I need to live

carnations

my blood

From "Les Etoiles de Novembre"
ANNE-MARIE DE BACKER
Translated from the French by Daniel Russell

I could only shout and laugh, as I trod the long juicy grass that stained my frock.... With tranquil pleasure you regarded my wild behavior, and when I stretched out my hand to reach those wild roses – you remember, the ones of such a tender pink – your hand broke the branch before I could, and you took off, one by one, the curved little thorns, coral-hued, claw shaped....And then you gave me the flowers, disarmed....

You gave me the flowers, disarmed....You gave me, so I could rest my panting self, the best place in the shade, under the Persian lilacs with their ripe bunches of flowers.

From *Sleepless Nights*
COLETTE

63

Of all flowers,
Methinks a rose is best.

From *Two Noble Kinsmen*
WILLIAM SHAKESPEARE

Among
of
green

stiff
old
bright

broken
branch
come

white
sweet
May

again

WILLIAM CARLOS WILLIAMS

Rose is a rose is a rose is a rose.

From *Sacred Emily*
GERTRUDE STEIN

May he who brings

flowers tonight,

have moonlight.

KIKAKU
Translated from the Japanese

somewhere i have never travelled, gladly beyond
any experience, your eyes have their silence:
in your most frail gesture are things which enclose me,
or which i cannot touch because they are too near

your slightest look easily will unclose me
though i have closed myself as fingers,
you open always petal by petal myself as Spring opens
[touching skillfully, mysteriously] her first rose

or if your wish be to close me, i and
my life will shut very beautifully, suddenly,
as when the heart of this flower imagines
the snow carefully everywhere descending;

nothing which we are to perceive in this world equals
the power of your intense fragility: whose texture
compels me with the colour of its countries,
rendering death and forever with each breathing

[i do not know what it is about you that closes
and opens; only something in me understands
the voice of your eyes is deeper than all roses]
nobody, not even the rain, has such small hands

e. e. cummings

See the flowers, the faithful of the earth

He who would carry them away into the

intimacy of sleep and would sleep

deeply with things – O how light he would return

different in the face of a different day, from

the common depth.

RAINER MARIA RILKE
Translated from the German by Angelloz

A *flower, and yet not a flower*

       Of mist, and yet not of mist

  At midnight she comes

    And at daybreak, leaves.

She comes like a spring dream, for how long?

She goes like morning dew, without a trace.

Po Chu-yi [772-846]
Translated from the Chinese by Eugene Eoyang